Anxiety

How to Cure Anxiety and Nervousness without Resorting to Dangerous Meds

Robert S. Lee

monetary loss due to the information herein, either directly or indirectly.

Respective authors own all copyrights not held by the publisher.

The information herein is offered for informational purposes solely, and is universal as so. The presentation of the information is without contract or any type of guarantee assurance.

The trademarks that are used are without any consent, and the publication of the trademark is without permission or backing by the trademark owner. All trademarks and brands within this book are for clarifying purposes only and are the owned by the owners themselves, not affiliated with this document.

Contents

Chapter 1. The Importance of Relieving Anxiety

When you let your anxiety run rampant, then you're not going to live a happy or healthy life. It is important that you control your anxiety, and you don't have to turn to over the counter or prescription drugs to do it. There are many natural remedies, habits, and tips that you can use to help. You can't cure it, but you can control it. Anxiety is a natural reaction to stressful situations, but there is no reason for it to cause you anxiety attacks. Anyone can actually have anxiety or experience anxiety, and it'll affect you no matter what type of life you live.

What Anxiety Can Cause:

It can be worse than an anxiety attack, but an anxiety attack is certainly nothing to laugh at. An anxiety attack can actually cause hives that can close up your airways, and you should never let your anxiety truly get that bad. Too much anxiety can also lead to depression, more stress, interrupt your sleep cycle, and even cause paranoia.

It can even lower your immune system. Your immune system is important so make sure it's up and running if you want to stay healthy. It can even cause binge eating if you don't know how to properly cope with your anxiety and the stress that it causes. You need to lower your anxiety if you want to make sure that you're able to handle the day. It can even affect your emotional state, which will cause a lack of confidence and interrupt your life. It can affect your judgement, interfere with school, work, and your relationships. If you're not being careful, then anxiety can lead you into depression, which will also disrupt your life.

Coping Naturally:

Anxiety is something that you'll never cure. So make sure that you're able to cope with it naturally if you want to be able to live a happy and healthy life. This goes from changing your environment to changing your habits, which are all discussed in the chapters to come. However, you'll also find that there are many natural and herbal remedies that you can use to help as well from teas to essential oils to body butter.

There is always something that you can take throughout the day that will help you. Of course, you'll find that there are many different solutions, but not all solutions will work for everyone. You need to experiment and find out which solutions work best for you. Many people find that it's a combination of things that is best if you want to truly control your anxiety. You need to employ methods that are both immediate and those that will help you in the long term, such as body butter that you can take with you.

When You Know It's a Problem:

You know anxiety is a problem when it starts to affect your sleep or interfere with your social or work life. You need to be able to function without feeling anxious or stressed throughout the day.

This is why you need these natural coping mechanisms and natural and herbal remedies. When you find yourself having issues with dealing with what life has to throw at you on a day to day basis, it's usually because of stress and anxiety. If you notice that you're depressed or have a poor outlook on life, it's also usually because of anxiety. If you're arguing and seem snappish even though you don't know why, it usually has to deal with anxiety. These are all clues to when anxiety is starting to get the best of you. Make sure that you start to employ coping mechanisms and herbal remedies immediately if you don't want your anxiety to get out of hand, which will also help to keep away anxiety attacks.

Chapter 2. Anxiety Relieving Essential Oils

Essential oil is a great way to relieve anxiety. Not every essential oil that is therapeutic grade, which is what is needed for an anxiety relieving or any beneficial effect, isn't always cheap. Of course, you'll find that essential oils go a long way, and they help you to achieve relief quickly. You can use a single essential oil or use an essential oil blend. You will want three essential oils in a blend, or you can just buy an anxiety blend for yourself. Knowing which essential oils work best will help you to determine if an essential oil blend is worth buying or not.

Essential Oil #1 Lavender

Lavender is a therapeutic essential oil that is usually easy to get ahold of, and it's not one of the more expensive essential oils. Lavender flowers are able to help with a lot of ailments, and they're a common herbal remedy. Of course, you'll find that the essential oil can be used effectively on its own. You can also use it to help you sleep since it is very easy to get ahold of, and all you need is one to two drops for migraines, anxiety, stress and to help sleep. Use a carrier oil, usually sweet almond or coconut. Of course, you can also just diffuse it throughout the room. Lavender is a middle or top note, depending on your blend.

Essential Oil #2 Wild Orange

Don't just get orange essential oil. If you want to make sure you have the right one, make sure that it says wild orange and that it's a therapeutic grade essential oil. It gives off a citrusy scent, and it's great at lifting your mood. That's exactly how it helps to make sure that your anxiety is taken care of. It helps you to think more positively and relax your mind. It helps with irritation, panic, nervousness, and even anger, relieving them almost instantly. You can rub it on the back of your neck or the bottoms of your feet for the best results. Use a carrier oil if needed. Like all essential oils, if you apply them directly to the skin your skin can suffer an irritation. Wild orange is a base note.

Essential Oil #3 Bergamot

Bergamot is an essential oil that many people don't think about, and it is also known for an almost citrusy smell. It can help you with any sudden mood swings or stress, which all contribute to anxiety. It is known to help you express your feelings, even if you have them pent up. It's an essential oil that is known to help you let go of whatever is keeping you depressed or causing your anxiety, and it's calming to the mind. Bergamot is a top note.

Essential Oil #4 Lemon

If you're looking for a cheap therapeutic essential oil that is going to still help with your anxiety, then lemon is always a good choice. One of the best parts is that it's a versatile essential oil, which is always helpful. It blends well with floral scents or citrusy fruits. It's uplifting and stimulating. It's certainly not an essential oil that will put you to sleep. You can actually use this by diffusing it through the room, but if you get the right essential oil, you can put it in your water. Just one to two drops, and it'll help. Lemon is a top note, but many people still use it as a middle note.

Essential Oil #5 Frankincense

Frankincense is known to slow your breathing and help with stress, anxiety, and even depression. It helps with fear and tension as well. It's commonly mixed with lavender for the best results, and it can help if you rub it on the back of your neck or the bottom of your feet. Of course, diffusing it in the room is also known to help with anxiety. Frankincense is a base note.

Essential Oil #6 Patchouli

Patchouli is a great way to stabilize your mind, as it helps to calm your emotions. That's why it's great for stress and anxiety. You can apply it to the base of your skull, or you can diffuse it throughout the room for the same benefit though less direct. Patchouli is a base note.

Essential Oil #7 Roman Chamomile

You've probably already heard of chamomile tea, but you'll find that roman chamomile essential oil is actually great at relieving both stress and anxiety. It can even stave off the effects of depression. It can smell sweet or fruity at times, and it has been known to help with muscle tension as well, which means it helps to relax your mind and your body. It can even help with ADD and insomnia. Roman chamomile is a middle note.

Essential Oil #8 Clary Sage

Clary sage is great at anxiety reduction, and it is commonly combined with lavender, rosemary, and even peppermint. It's not a cure for anxiety, but it has an incredibly soothing effect. It's great at calming your mind, and it's known to help with depression as well as stress. Clary sage is not commonly used on its own, and it has the best results when done in a blend. Clary sage is also a middle note.

Essential Oil #9 Jasmine

If you're looking for an essential oil that is intoxicating and florally, then you're going to want to try jasmine. It helps with anxiety, but it is one of the more expensive oils that you'd be getting for anxiety. A therapeutic grade jasmine oil can be slightly painful. Just remember not to get a cheaper grade, or it won't actually help you battle anxiety. Jasmine essential oil is another middle note.

Essential #10 Sandalwood

Sandalwood essential oil has a very woodsy smell to it, and it's considered a more manly scent to help get rid of anxiety. It is also known to help to improve the quality of sleep you get and help you get on a better sleep cycle. Getting enough sleep also helps to make sure that you're reducing anxiety effectively. Sandalwood essential oil is a base note.

How to Blend Essential Oils:

Of course, if you're going to be using essential oils, you need to know how to blend them unless you're using them just on their own. Blending essential oils will usually provide a much stronger effect, and it can help you to battle depression and anxiety. First you need to ask yourself what result you want to identify what oils that you should blend together. In this case your end result is something that will help to relieve the anxiety you're feeling. You're going to need to blend them based on their category, such as woodsy, minty, medicinal, citrus, oriental, and spicy and so on.

Blend based on what you think will go together to make a delightful scent that has a bottom, top and middle note. Each note is based on how quickly it evaporates, and by blending the notes you know that your essential oil blend will last a while. For any beginner it's recommended that you start with three oils to blend properly. Make thirty percent of your oil your top note, fifty percent your middle note and twenty percent your base note. Stick to that ratio and you're sure to get a blend that will work. Of course, you can always buy blends that will help you to relieve anxiety as well, which will help you if you don't feel comfortable blending your own essential oils for anxiety relief.

Chapter 3. Curing Anxiety with the Right Tea

Having a warm drink is known to help calm you down, and anxiety is no different. Tea can help, and when you have the right tea it can help even more. Most of these tea recipes can actually be drank hot or cold, but drinking them throughout the day is more helpful than just drinking them once a day. If you're drinking them cold, many people prefer to make them in advance. Incorporating teas into your daily routine is easy, but remember that if you want them cold you'll need to make them in advance. You can make a larger batch if you're icing it, so that you can use it throughout the day.

Tea #1 Lavender Iced Tea

You don't always need a hot tea for it to work on your anxiety. Sometimes you just need something that is going to help you by making sure you relax, cold or not. That's exactly what this lavender remedy is going to help with. Lavender is a relaxing scent and it has a relaxing effect on the body when ingested. Dried lavender is easy to get ahold of, but fresh lavender will also work.

Ingredients:

1. 12 Teabags of Your Favorite Tea

2. 2 ½ Teaspoons Dried Lavender

3. 3 ½ Teaspoons Honey, Raw

Directions:

1. Take a gallon of water and bring it to a boil. Allow the lavender and tea bags too steep for twenty to thirty minutes after taking the water off heat. Strain out the lavender and take out the tea bags.

2. Stir in your honey, and then put in the refrigerator to cool. Serve it over ice.

Tea #2 Night Time Lemon Balm

Lemon balm tea is great if you're looking for something that will help you to get to sleep and reduce anxiety quickly. It does have a calming, sedative effect, which is why you should take it before bed. Do not take it in the morning. Your stress will melt away with this tea, leaving you less anxious and ready for a good night's sleep. Of course, you can add honey to taste.

Ingredients:

1. 1 Cup Water
2. 2 Teaspoons Honey, Raw
3. 2 Tablespoons Lemon Balm, Dried

Directions:

1. Just boil the water, and then take it off heat. Leave your lemon balm to steep for ten to twelve minutes.

2. Strain it out, and then add in your honey and drink warm.

Tea #3 Lemon Balm Blend

This makes four cups of tea, and if you want to make an individual cup, you'll want to take a rounded tablespoon of the blend. It makes ¼ cup of tea blend. The orange peel and rosehips are great at helping to make sure that you have the right vitamin C to allow you to feel healthier while the lemon balm and lavender will help you to melt your anxiety away. The oat straw is also known to help relieve anxiety.

Ingredients:

1. 2 Tablespoons Lemon Balm, Dried
2. 1 Cup Water
3. 1 Tablespoon Oat straw
4. 2 Teaspoons Rosehips, Dried & Seedless
5. 1 ½ Teaspoons Orange Peel, Dried & Grated
6. ½ Teaspoon Lavender Buds, Dried

Directions:

1. Take a tablespoon of the blend, and pour boiling water over it. It should be one

cup of water, and then you'll want to let it steep for twenty minutes to twenty-five minutes. Strain out the herbs, and then add honey to taste. You can drink it warm or cold.

Tea #4 Peppermint Tea

Peppermint tea is known to help with anxiety as well. It also helps to lift and stabilize your mood. Lemon juice is also known to help, and it'll even help with your digestive system. It's an easy tea to make, and getting dried peppermint leaves is not that hard.

Ingredients:

1. 2 Teaspoons Peppermint Leaves, Dried

2. ½ Teaspoon Peppermint Extract

3. 2 Teaspoons Honey, Raw

4. ½ Teaspoon Lemon Juice, Fresh

Directions:

1. Take a cup of water and boil it, and then take it off the heat. Steep your peppermint leaves in it, adding in your lemon juice and extract.

2. Strain out your herbs after letting it steep for fifteen to twenty minutes, and then add in your honey.

Tea #5 Lavender & Chamomile

Lavender and chamomile are both known to reduce stress, and you can use the dried flower buds to make it. They're easy to get ahold of, and it'll help reduce your stress immediately.

However, it's also great to help with sleep, so you'll find that it's best to take it in the evening.

Ingredients:

1. 2 Teaspoons Lavender Buds, Dried
2. 1 Teaspoon Chamomile Flowers, Dried
3. 1 Teaspoon Honey, Raw

Directions:

1. Boil a cup of water, and then put in your lavender and chamomile flowers, letting it steep for six to eight minutes.
2. Strain them out, and then mix in the honey.

Tea #6 Basil

Basil tea is great for stress and anxiety, and you usually have it in your cabinet already. Of course, you'll also find that you can use fresh or dried basil, and fresh basil is quite easy to grow. Herbs flourish, and they're wonderful if you're trying to grow them in containers. Basil even has the added benefit of helping with stomachaches and headaches.

Ingredients:

1. 1 ½ Teaspoons Basil, Dried
2. 1 Teaspoon Honey, Raw

Directions:

1. Take a cup of boiling water, and then pour it over the basil. Let it steep for seven to ten minutes.

2. Strain out the basil, and then add honey to taste. Of course, you can always add a half teaspoon of lemon juice as well for flavor.

Tea #7 Mint & Lavender Iced Tea

This is a great cold tea recipe that will help you with any stress and anxiety that you're having. Mint, lavender, and lemon is going to reduce your anxiety. It's easy to make, and you can make a half gallon to a gallon at a time. Drink it throughout the day for the best results. You can add a few tea bags of your favorite tea for a stronger taste if desired.

Ingredients:

1. 4 Tablespoons Mint Leaves, Fresh
2. ¼ Cup Lavender Buds, Dried
3. 1 Teaspoon Lemon Juice, Fresh
4. 3 Tablespoons Honey, Raw

Directions:

1. Take a half a gallon of water and boil it, adding in the mint leaves, lemon juice, and lavender buds. Let it simmer for seven to twelve minutes.

2. Take it off heat, and strain out the herbs. Add in honey while still warm so that it'll help to dissolve it. Make sure it's dissolved before putting it up to cool. Serve it over ice.

Tea #8 Rosemary & Lemon

This is an earthy blend, and the honey is a great way to sweeten it. Rosemary is easy to grow, and you can use fresh rosemary if desired.

41

Lemon juice will also help to work in a pinch. These two ingredients are all you need to get your anxiety down, but it's best to drink a few cups a day.

Ingredients:

1. 2 Tablespoons Rosemary, Dried
2. 1 Small Lemon, Sliced
3. 2 Teaspoons Honey, Raw

Directions:

1. Boil a cup of water, and then add in the rosemary. Squeeze the lemon slices, and then add it into steep. Take the water off

the heat and let steep for eight to ten minutes.

2. Add in honey after straining out the herbs, and drink while warm or chill if desired.

Chapter 4. Bath Salts that Really Help

Taking a hot bath will actually help to make sure that you relax and relieve anxiety and stress. You'll find that it's easy to make your own bath salts, and they make great gifts as well. Just keep them in an airtight glass container, and use them whenever you feel anxiety pressing in on you. Warm baths are even known to help you sleep, which can relieve anxiety as well.

Bath Salt #1 Bedtime Salts

Having the right sleep schedule is going to help make sure that your anxiety disappear. You'll find that being on the right schedule will help you to relieve your anxiety and face the day with a little more confidence. Lavender essential oils are known to help you with anxiety, as stated before. Epsom salts are a great way to relax your muscles and relieve tension as well.

Ingredients:

1. 5-8 Drops Lavender Essential Oil
2. ¼ Cup Lavender Buds, Dried & Crushed
3. 1 Tablespoon Coconut Oil
4. ½ Cup Sea Salt, Medium Coarse

5. 1 Cup Epsom Salts

Directions:

1. Combine all the ingredients together, and store them in an airtight glass container.

Bath Salt #2 Stress & Anxiety Melting

Roses are known to uplift your mood, and vanilla essential oil does the same thing. With these uplifting scents paired with the anxiety relief that lavender can bring, you have a bath salt that is sure to help with anxiety, depression, and stress. It's even a great way to relax after a stressful day because of the way

Epsom salts help to relieve the tension in your muscles.

Ingredients:

1. ½ Cup Rose Petals, Dried & Crushed

2. 1 Cup Epsom Salts

3. 6-8 Drops Lavender Essential Oil

4. 3-5 Drops Vanilla Essential Oil

5. 2-4 Drops Rose Essential Oil

Directions:

1. Mix all ingredients together, and then put the mixture in an airtight container.

Bath Salt #3 An Uplifting Mix

This is a bath salt mix that will help you to uplift your mood, and it'll help any sore muscles that you may be having issues with as well. Eucalyptus essential oil is great for sore muscles, and peppermint is great at chasing away anxiety and stress, just like the lavender. You can always add more lavender or peppermint depending on your tastes.

Ingredients:

1. 1 Cup Epsom Salts
2. ¼ Cup Sea Salt, Fine
3. 4-6 Drops Eucalyptus Essential Oil
4. 8-10 Drops Peppermint Essential Oil
5. 6-8 Drops Lavender Essential Oil

Directions:

1. Mix everything together, making sure all essential oils are mixed all the way through. Store in an airtight container.

Bath Salt #4 Chamomile

You already know that chamomile flowers and roman chamomile essential oil is known to help with stress and anxiety. Another wonderful way to utilize that is through bath salts, and it's a great way to establish a proper sleeping cycle as well. A hot bath already helps with sleep. The dried flowers even make it a beautiful mixture, which helps if you want to package it as a gift.

Ingredients:

1. 1 Cup Epsom Salts
2. ½ Cup Sea Salt, Medium Coarse
3. ½ Cup Chamomile Flowers, Dried
4. 10-15 Drops Roman Chamomile Essential Oil
5. ¼ Cup Baking Soda, Aluminum Free

Direction:

1. Combine everything together, and mix well. Make sure everything is put into airtight glass container for storage.

Bath Salt #5 Anxiety Free Mix

Bergamot, lavender, and wild orange are all known to help relieve anxiety, and it'll help your mind and body to calm down when you're using it in a hot, relaxing bath. It'll help you get ready for bed or get ready for the day, and when the oils are blended together in the salt, it helps to create a wonderful scent that you're sure to enjoy.

Ingredients:

1. 1 Cup Epsom Salts
2. ½ Cup Sea Salt, Coarse
3. 6-8 Drops Bergamot Essential Oil
4. 2-5 Drops Lavender Essential Oil
5. 8-10 Drops Wild Orange Essential Oil

6. ¼ Cup Lavender Buds, Dried & Crushed

Directions:

1. Mix everything together, making sure that your essential oils are thoroughly combined. Store in an airtight container.

Bath Salt #6 Citrus Relaxation Blend

This is a great bath salt that is going to promote relaxation because of the green tea leaves, which is known to help you to relax like Epsom salts. As well as the lemon and wild orange essential oils. Make sure that your green tea leaves are crushed.

Ingredients:

1. 2 Tablespoons Green Tea Leaves

2. 10-15 Drops Wild Orange Essential Oil

3. 4-6 Drops Lemon Essential Oil

4. 1 Cup Epsom Salts

5. ½ Cup Sea Salt, Fine

Directions:

1. Take a mortar and pestle, making sure to crush your green tea leaves, and then mix everything together. Store in an airtight, glass container until you're ready to use this bath salt mix.

Chapter 5. Body Butters to Help You Calm Down

Body butters can actually help you to calm down and relieve any anxiety that you may be feeling. It's easy to apply, as it works just like lotion. It is also something that you can package and use as a gift, and often you'll want to put it in an airtight glass container, which is easy to decorate.

Body Butter #1 Whipped Magnesium

Magnesium is great at relieving anxiety, especially in its oil form. That's why this body butter concentrates mostly on magnesium oil.

However, you can use an essential oil of your choice or leave it out entirely. Wild orange is also great at helping with anxiety, but you can add a different one of your choice as well.

Ingredients:

1. ¼ Cup Coconut Oil, Extra Virgin

2. ¼ Cup Magnesium Oil

3. ½ Cup Cocoa Butter, Refined

4. 10 Drops Wild Orange Essential Oil

Directions:

1. Melt your coconut oil and cocoa butter over a double boiler. Once melted and

combined, put it in a medium bowl and let cool to room temperature.

2. Whip it together and add in the oil. Place it in the refrigerator for twenty to twenty-five minutes

3. Take back out, and whip again until fluffy.

4. Put in airtight containers for storage, preferably glass.

Body Butter #2 Lavender Mix

Coconut oil is great for your skin, and it's a great base for your body butter as well. All you need to do is mix in an essential oil that is known to help with anxiety relief, such as lavender. You don't want to mix in lavender buds, even when ground, because it'll make the body butter less smooth, which isn't the texture you want.

Ingredients:

1. 10 Drops Lavender Essential Oil

2. 1 Cup Coconut Oil, Extra Virgin

3. 2-6 Drops Peppermint Essential Oil

Directions:

1. Melt the coconut oil in a double boiler, and then combine the essential oils. Put it in a bowl to let cool to room temperature. Whisk.

2. Let sit in the refrigerator for twenty to twenty-five minutes, and then take it back out to whip until fluffy.

3. Put it in glass jars.

Body Butter #3 Rosemary & Clary Sage

This is a more earthy body butter, but it still does the trick when it comes to anxiety. Both rosemary and Clary Sage essential oils are great at helping to make sure that you chase your anxiety away quickly and effectively. It's a light scent, and the coconut oil makes sure that the body butter is smooth.

Ingredients:

1. 1 Cup Coconut Oil, Extra Virgin

2. 8-10 Drops Clary Sage Essential Oil

3. 4-6 Drops Rosemary Essential Oil

Directions:

1. Mix everything together in a double boiler until everything is melted.

2. Move it to a bowl so that it can cool down to room temperature and whip it.

3. Put in the refrigerator for twenty to thirty minutes, and then whip it again before moving it to airtight containers to keep until you're ready to use or give it away as a gift.

Body Butter #4 Herbal Blend

This herbal blend is great if you're looking for something that will really help with anxiety. What most people don't know is that basil essential oil is also great at helping to relieve stress and anxiety, just like rosemary. With the wild orange and lemon paired with it you get a very earthy and citrusy blend. The Shea butter and coconut oil make a smooth but thick body butter that will moisturize your skin and uplift your mood while banishing stress.

Ingredients:

1. 1 Cup Shea Butter, Raw
2. ¼ Cup Coconut Oil, Extra Virgin
3. 7-10 Lemon Essential Oil

4. 10-12 Drops Wild Orange Essential Oil

5. 5-8 Drops Rosemary Essential Oil

6. 7-10 Drops Basil Essential Oil

Directions:

1. Take a double boiler and melt your coconut oil and Shea butter together. Make sure to continue stirring or your Shea butter will become gritty. When melted, put it in a bowl and take it off of heat.

2. Mix in your essential oils, and whip it.

3. Place the mixture in the refrigerator for twenty to thirty minutes or until firm. Whip it again until it is light and fluffy,

and then spoon in the mixture into glass jars.

Body Butter #5 Vanilla & Basil Blend

Vanilla is great at stabilizing your mood, and if your mood isn't stable, then you're much more likely to get anxiety attacks and your stress levels will sky rocket. When added to the sweet and yet earthy tone of basil essential oil, which isn't one of the more expensive essential oils then you'll find that your anxiety will start to lessen immediately. It'll even help to improve blood circulation.

Ingredients:

1. 8-10 Drops Vanilla Essential Oil

2. 6-8 Drops Rosemary Essential Oil

3. 1 Cup Coconut Oil, Extra Virgin

4. ½ Cup Shea Butter, Raw

Directions:

1. Take a double boiler, and put in the Shea butter and coconut oil. Melt together, and stir regularly so that the Shea butter doesn't get gritty. Once melted and mixed together, take it and put it in a separate bowl.

2. Mix in your essential oils with a hand mixer, whipping it some.

3. Put the entire bowl in a refrigerator, and let sit for twenty-five to thirty minutes. It should be somewhat firm when you take it out. You're going to want to whip it until it's light and fluffy. Then you can spoon it into different containers to use later.

Body Butter #6 Lemon & Rosemary

You already know that rosemary and lemon oil will help with your anxiety, and when added together it makes a unique and fresh blend. It'll help to make your stress less, and it's the perfect spring or summer scent.

Ingredients:

1. 10-12 Drops Lemon Essential Oil

2. 6-8 Drops Rosemary Essential Oil

3. 1 Cup Coconut Oil, Extra Virgin

4. ½ Cup Cocoa Butter, Raw

Directions:

1. Take a double boiler, putting the coconut oil and cocoa butter together. Make sure to stir occasionally while they're melting. This will keep anything from being gritty. Once melted, take it from the double boiler and put it in a medium to large bowl to mix in your essential oils.

2. Put in the refrigerator to firm up. This will usually take twenty-five to thirty

minute. Then, take it out of the refrigerator and whip it until smooth and fluffy. Then you can place it in airtight containers until you're ready to use it or give it as a gift.

Chapter 6. Herbal Remedies to Get Rid of it Fast

There are still more herbal remedies that you can use to help you control and get rid of your anxiety. Anxiety brings down your mood, affects your relationships, and even effects your productivity. Don't let anxiety control your life, and these herbal remedies are easy to incorporate into your life.

Remedy #1 Golden Milk Recipe

Not only does golden milk help with anxiety, depression, and stress it can also help with the cold and flu. It's easy to make, and it's a cold drink that you can use. It's an herbal remedy that will help you to relax and let go of anything that is causing the anxiety and stress.

Ingredients:

1. 1 Cups Milk, Whole
2. 2 Teaspoons Honey, Raw
3. 1/8 Teaspoon Black Pepper, Ground
4. ½ Teaspoon Turmeric, Dried
5. ½ Teaspoon Ginger, Dried

Directions:

1. Heat the milk in a saucepan over medium heat. Make sure to stir so it doesn't stick or burn.

2. Add in the ginger, turmeric, and black pepper. Stir well and let it all begin to simmer again. Allow it to simmer for another two or three minutes, and then take it off heat. Add in your honey, and put it into a cup to drink warm or cold.

Remedy #2 An Essential Oil Blend

You already know that essential oils are a great way to go to get rid of stress and anxiety, and this blend is perfect and easy to make. If you don't have coconut oil, you can use sweet almond oil for results as well. Some people even use olive oil as a carrier oil for this essential oil blend.

Ingredients:

1. 1 Teaspoon Coconut Oil, Extra Virgin
2. 1-2 Drops Bergamot Essential Oil
3. 2-3 Drops Wild Orange Essential Oil
4. 3-4 Drops Lavender Essential Oil

Directions:

Mix everything together, and apply it to the forearms. You can diffuse it in the air as well, but it works best when applied directly to your forearms. You can use this once or twice daily.

Remedy #3 Rose Water

Roses are medicinal, and many people don't know that. However, proper rose water can help to make sure that your anxiety slips away quickly and easily. Of course, wild roses are always best, but if you're buying store bought roses, make sure they're organic. You don't want any harmful pesticides in your rose water if you want it to help.

Ingredients:

1. 20-30 Rose Petals, Fresh
2. 3 Cups Water

Directions:

1. Make sure to rinse your rose petals off, and then put them in the water in a saucepan. Put it over medium heat. Cover it. Let simmer until all of the color is gone from the rose petals. Remember to stir occasionally.

2. Strain the petals out and put the water in an airtight container.

3. To use, make sure that you apply it to your skin, usually around the face. It has an added benefit of being a toner.

Remedy #4 Herbal Foot Bath

This is a foot bath that is great for relieving your stress and anxiety. It'll even help to get rid of depression. Epsom salts will relax you, and the roses, wild orange essential oil, and lavender oil will help to make sure your foot bath is a relaxing one. Do it once daily, and you'll notice that your anxiety starts to melt away.

Ingredients:

1. 10-15 Drops Lavender Essential Oil
2. 6-8 Drops Wild Orange Essential Oil
3. ¼ Cup Rose Petals, Dried
4. ½ Cup Epsom Salts
5. 3 Cups Water

Directions:

1. Boil your water, and then add in the herbs. Reduce to a simmer and simmer for twenty to twenty-five minutes. Take it and put it in a foot bath, adding in your Epsom salts.

2. Let cool a little, and soak your feet for twenty to thirty minutes.

Remedy #5 Anxiety Relief Balm

Cedar wood is also great at helping to reduce anxiety, and it's an essential oil used in this wonderful balm. It's not as thin as a lotion, and it's easier to carry around as it's more compact. A little goes a long way, and you can use it throughout the day to make sure your anxiety stays away.

Ingredients:

1. ½ Ounce Beeswax, Grated
2. 6 Tablespoons Olive Oil, Extra Virgin
3. 1 Tablespoon Magnesium Oil
4. 15-20 Drops Lavender Essential Oil
5. 10-12 Drops Cedar wood Essential Oil
6. 10-15 Drops Vanilla Essential Oil

Directions:

1. Take your olive oil and beeswax, melting it in a double boiler. Use low heat, and stir well until it's completely combined.

Add in all oils, and mix in as you take it off the heat.

2. Pour into containers to cool. Use it on your pulse points such as your wrists and collar bone when you are feeling anxious or stressed out. You can use it throughout the day for the best results.

Chapter 7. Natural Habits to Rid Yourself of Anxiety

What you do or do not do throughout the day will also affect your level of anxiety. It's important to have habits that help you to calm down, release stress, and keep anxiety at bay. It'll even help to stave off depression and make you a happier, healthier you. Many of these habits are easy to use and incorporate into your life, and they even help out with your overall health. Don't forget to stack your habits. There is no reason to employ just one habit to help you gain a little more control over your anxiety.

Habit #1 Find Time to be Grateful

This may not seem like a habit that is hard, but it's important that you find something to be grateful for throughout the day if you want to be anxiety free. Many people say that they're being grateful without actually putting time into it. You need to be grateful even when everything is crashing down around you if you really want it to work. This includes if people are being rude or that you're surrounded by unhappiness. There is always something that you can find yourself being grateful for, but sometimes you'll need to think about it. Be grateful and smile, and it can help your anxiety and stress to melt away.

Habit #2 Concentrate on One Thing at a Time

Never concentrate on too many things if you don't want to fall prey to anxiety. Anxiety comes from feeling insecure or overwhelmed, which is easy if you're trying to multi-task and can't handle it. Even if you think you can handle it, it's actually better if you concentrate on one thing at a time. This will also help to breed a sense of accomplishment as you mark off one thing and then the next, and that will help you to feel less stressed out.

Habit #3 Be Decisive

Being decisive helps to make sure that you're certain about your next move. Being certain about your next move will help to make sure that you know what you're doing. Anxiety is often stemmed from not understanding what you should do next. It'll make it hard for you to move on throughout the day with certainty. If you are certain, then anxiety will start to diminish.

Habit #4 Make a List

This is helpful for the same reason that being decisive is. If you know what you're doing, then there is no reason to be anxious or fearful of what is going to happen next. You will also know what to accomplish, and this will keep you from feeling like you haven't accomplished anything that day. It'll also keep things from piling up on you. When responsibilities start to pile up on you, then you're much more likely to feel overwhelmed. It can have a negative impact on what you're feeling or if you think you can get through the day. By taking that overwhelming feeling out of the equation, you're more likely to be confident, happier, and anxious free.

Habit #5 Meditate Occasionally

Meditating everyday would be best, but most people can't find the time to do that. However, it is what you should strive for. Meditation is known to help relieve any feelings of anxiousness, stress, or even depression. Any sort of meditation is important. You can choose what type of meditation you want, and it'll help to make sure that you are starting to center yourself. When you find your center, you are erasing your stress and anxiousness.

It helps you to accept your emotions and what's bothering you, and it can even help to relieve tension from your muscles. Even just a breathing meditation is best. Many people find it helpful to do so in the morning or in the evening, but you can really do meditation any time of day, and you don't have to be sitting with your legs crossed. Make sure you're in a quiet area with comfortable clothing where you aren't worried of being interrupted.

Habit #6 Distract Yourself

Sometimes everyone needs a good distraction, and that's because a good distraction can keep anxiety at bay. Sometimes, you don't need too much room to think. If you have been thinking too much, you're more than likely overthinking. Erase the fear by distracting yourself with a hobby or if you're being too anxious about something. Reading, embroidery, sewing, wood burning or anything with your hands is usually best. It'll help to make sure that you're not letting anxiety take over and rule your life.

Habit #7 Use a Mantra

Sometimes, when all else fails a mantra can be incredibly useful. It's best that you make your own mantra that will help you. A mantra is a reassurance to yourself, so having a few of them is okay as well. Tell yourself that you will be happy or healthy. Tell yourself that you are confident or anxiety free. As you repeat it, you'll find that it becomes more and more helpful. Often, repeating a mantra in front of a mirror will help to make sure that you are really believing what you're saying. You can say your mantra during any stressful situation in the day, and you can tell yourself before you go out for the day as well. This will help to boost your confidence.

Habit #8 Dress to Impress Yourself

Everyone knows the phrase to dress to impress, but you need to be dressing to impress yourself if you want to relieve anxiety immediately. If you feel confident in what you're wearing, then you will feel less anxious about the day. Confidence directly relates to helping to make sure that you know what you're doing and how to go about your day. You don't always need to be in business attire, but you should never wear something you don't like or that undermines your confidence.

Habit #9 Remind Yourself It'll Pass

Sometimes you need a reminder if you want to feel better. This means that you may need to remind yourself that even a bad situation is going to go away. Reminding yourself something is going to pass will help you to get through it and gain a more positive outlook on a situation. Otherwise, you may feel hopeless. Hopelessness is going to be your enemy when trying to get rid of anxiety.

Habit #10 The Right Sleep Cycle

Finding the right amount of sleep is going to help you to feel less anxious overall as well. It'll help you to feel like you can handle the day, and it'll help to relieve stress if you're well rested. This means that you should be getting eight to nine hours as an adult. This means that you're going to want to wake up and get up at around the same time every day. Establishing a routine is also proven to help with stress and anxiety as a whole. It's also important to be asleep while it's still dark out. If you sleep during the day, you're more likely to have nightmares, which will only contribute to stress and anxiety.

Chapter 8. Bonus Ways to Help You Control Anxiety

There are still many natural and herbal ways to help you control your anxiety, so there is no reason to use over the counter medication or prescription drugs. Take control of your anxiety to take your life back, and you'll find that it can help you to live happier while being healthier. Don't let anxiety rule your life.

Tip #1 Take Time to Yourself

If you really want to help with your stress and anxiety, one of the best and natural methods to do so is to take time to yourself. It doesn't really matter what you're doing, and it's more than just a distraction. You should have time in your day when you can focus on yourself, and it'll help to ease the anxiety away. It can be for yoga, music, massage, or any relaxation technique you can think of. Thirty minutes to an hour is recommended, and many people like to do it as a way to wind down before bed, which also helps you to get better sleep.

Tip #2 Count to Ten

When you're in the moment where something is making you incredibly anxious, you're going to want to take a moment to let that anxiety go if you want to assess the situation with a clear head. Sometimes it's as simple as closing your eyes and taking deep breaths as you count to ten. If you're still anxious, count back down to zero. When you open your eyes, you should be able to release your anxiety, and it'll help you to address the situation at hand.

Tip #3 Accept Lack of Control

You cannot always manage your life, and sometimes you have to accept that. There are many things that you can change, and there are many things that you cannot. Accepting that there are some things you can't will help to make sure that you don't feel too stressed about what can't be changed. This allows you to redirect your attention to something you can so you don't waste your energy.

Tip #4 Allow for Humor

Everyone know that when you're in a bad mood you don't always want to laugh, but sometimes you need to. A good laugh is a great remedy to chase away anxiety, and it'll help you to feel better almost instantly. Being around someone who can make you laugh is always a good thing, but you may find that finding your own sense of humor will help you out more in the long run. You need to find humor even in the bad, as laughing and smiling is the best way to control stress and anxiety.

Tip #5 Establish a Routine

A routine certainly isn't for everyone, but if you're having issues with anxiety and stress piling up on you, then you may want to establish a routine. It's often best if you make sure that you have something you can count on. Even your anxiety relieving habits can become a routine. For example, a bed time routine is going to help you, but eating your meals at a certain time is known to help as well.

Establishing something you can rely on helps to relieve uncertainty.

Tip #6 Learn Your Triggers

If you're becoming anxious a lot, you may want to try and learn what your triggers are. Everyone has a trigger. Sometimes it's people, certain places, or even food. Notice your triggers, and then eliminate them from your life. There is no reason to allow anything to trigger your anxiety, as it can ruin the normalcy of your life. If you don't know how to identify your triggers, you're going to want to keep a journal. This will help you to make sure that you're able to identify them.

Tip #7 Take Away Negative Influences

You need to be careful who you're with if you want to find a way to relieve your anxiety. Anxiety can compound when you have too much negativity in your life. Usually this is because of the negative influences in your life, so make sure that you aren't surrounding yourself with negative people. It can even lead to chronic depression if you aren't doing something to get rid of the negativity in your life. If you cannot avoid the negative person, then try to minimize your time with them as much as possible.

Tip #8 Sweat It Out

Sometimes you need to just sweat out your frustration. Exercise is the way to go. It's usually best if you exercise for at least thirty minutes a day for five days a week. You can go for a walk, a jog, take up kickboxing, or just head to the gym. It doesn't matter how you're exercising, but exercise can help you.

Remember:

No matter what remember that you can do something about your anxiety naturally. There is no reason to feel hopeless. There is no reason to let it rule your life. There are long term solutions if you create a routine that will help you control it. Of course, many of these remedies are a short term solution as well, since they work quickly and effectively.